Game Design

CHERRY LAKE PUBLISHING • ANN ARBOR, MICHIGAN

by Greg Austic

CHERRY LAKE Publishing

A Note to Adults: Please review the instructions for the activities in this book before allowing children to do them. Be sure to help them with any activities you do not think they can safely complete on their own.

A Note to Kids: Be sure to ask an adult for help with these activities when you need it. Always put your safety first!

Published in the United States of America by Cherry Lake Publishing
Ann Arbor, Michigan
www.cherrylakepublishing.com

Series Editor: Kristin Fontichiaro
Photo Credits: Cover and pages 1, 18, 23, 25, 26, 27, 29, courtesy of Michigan Makers; page 4, ©Richard Elzey/www.flickr.com/CC-BY-2.0; page 5, ©compujeramey/www.flickr.com/CC-BY-2.0; pages 6, 16, and 19, ©woodleywonderworks/www.flickr.com/CC-BY-2.0; page 7, ©Neeta Lind/www.flickr.com/CC-BY-2.0; page 8, ©John-Morgan/www.flickr.com/CC-BY-2.0; page 9, ©tuchodi/www.flickr.com/CC-BY-2.0; page 12, ©North Charleston/www.flickr.com/CC-BY-SA-2.0; page 15, ©karpidis/www.flickr.com/CC-BY-2.0; page 20, ©Will Folsom/www.flickr.com/CC-BY-2.0

Library of Congress Cataloging-in-Publication Data
Austic, Greg.
  Game design/by Greg Austic.
     pages cm.—(Makers as innovators) (Innovation library)
  Includes bibliographical references and index.
  ISBN 978-1-62431-142-0 (lib. bdg.)—ISBN 978-1-62431-208-3 (e-book)—ISBN 978-1-62431-274-8 (pbk.)
  1. Video games—Design—Vocational guidance—Juvenile literature. 2. Computer games—Design—Vocational guidance. I. Title.
  GV1469.3.A92 2013
   794.8—dc23   2013004924

Cherry Lake Publishing would like to acknowledge the work of The Partnership for 21st Century Skills. Please visit www.p21.org for more information.

Printed in the United States of America
Corporate Graphics Inc.
July 2013
CLFA13

◆ 21st Century Skills INNOVATION LIBRARY

Contents

Chapter 1

What Are Games?

magine you are throwing a ball against a wall. Would you call that activity a game? While it may be fun, it's not really a game. Now imagine throwing a ball into a hoop. That's closer, but it is still not quite a game. Now give yourself two points every time you get the ball in the hoop. Draw a big box on the floor that you must stay within to score. First person to score 10 points wins! Aha! That sounds like basketball, which is definitely a game!

Is making a basket considered a game?

Most games have all of these elements: rules, outcomes, and conditions for ending the game.

How did we turn throwing a ball into a game? We added rules (two points per shot) and **outcomes** (winning and losing). We decided when those outcomes would happen (first to reach 10 points wins). Most games have all of these elements: rules, outcomes, and conditions for ending the game. Some games have two of the three. Together, these elements are called the game mechanics. When the

It is often difficult to explain why some games are more fun than others.

mechanics are in place, players can develop **tactics** and **strategies**. Then all kinds of interesting stuff starts to happen!

Great game designers can mix game mechanics, stories, and art together to give players an awesome experience—something really fun. But what is fun? This question may sound silly, but no one knows what fun actually is. People in the toy and game industry spend their whole lives trying to understand and predict how and when fun will happen, but they still don't always get it right. For example, in 1982, Atari created a video game based on the hugely success-ful movie *E.T. The Extra-Terrestrial*. Even though it cost $25 million to develop, it is now considered one of the worst video games of all time. Millions of unsold game cartridges were buried in a landfill because no one wanted to buy them!

The next time you play a game, think about the emotions you are feeling. Are you happy? Excited? Proud? Something else? Now try to figure out why the game is making you feel this way. Is it the gameplay or the art? Is it the story or the characters? Is it everything

What do you like best about your favorite games?

all at once? Understanding how a game triggers your feelings is a good first step toward being a game designer and being able to understand what fun is.

Ask a Game Designer

What should you invent if you want a shot at getting your game published? Start by looking at the games currently for sale on store shelves. Ask yourself what is missing. For example, you see five card games for sale and three of them also have dice versions. Maybe you can invent dice versions for the other two card games! Pay attention to how much stuff is in the game for the money you spend. A game that's too expensive to produce will not get published. Next, make sure your game plays well for the same age and number of players as other games on the store shelf. For example, games that require exactly four players generally do not get published. Finally, your game has to be tons of fun to play, and tons of fun to play again and again. If people besides your friends and family like playing your game, then you might just have a great game in the making!

Garry Donner is a successful game designer and entrepreneur who has published hundreds of board games over the past 25 years. Fifteen of his games have sold more than a million copies worldwide!

Chapter 2

The World Is Full of Games

Y ou probably know about video games, board games, outdoor games, and card games. But the world is full of other kinds of games, too. Adults call them by different names, but they are still games because they are systems with **incentives** to behave in a certain way.

A simple deck of playing cards can be used to play many different games.

The Stock Market: A Big, Expensive Guessing Game

A stock market is a system that allows people to buy or sell shares of ownership in companies across the world. The total value of all of the world's stock markets is a whopping $36.6 trillion! Even though the stock market is very valuable, it is designed like a simple game. Imagine you bought stock in companies. Your stock's value rises if other people also buy that stock. It goes down if other people sell that stock. If you want your stock to go up and become more valuable, you have to guess today what everyone else will be buying tomorrow. Buy low, sell high, and make money. It is the real world, but it has all the features of a game. Yep, this is the real world. Weird, right?

School: A Game of Who Can Get the Higher Test Score

You are probably an expert in playing the school game. So try this: ask some adults what the outcome of school should be. Is it to make kids smart or to give them opportunities? Is it to prepare them for college or to keep them busy while their parents work? Is it something else entirely? What incentives do schools use to get you to do things you may not want to do? Think about a student who doesn't want to do the homework. How could school change the game and convince that person to care about the outcomes and play by the rules? If you designed the school game, how would it work?

Marketing: The Game of Getting More Paying Customers

Companies are always looking for clever ways to get you to buy their products. From secret decoders in your breakfast cereal box to tear-off game pieces in the fast-food drive-through, companies use the excitement and competition of games to entice you to buy their products. Of course, as a game designer, you aren't fooled, right?

Military Strategy: A Game of Controlling Land, People, and Stuff

Military operations have a lot in common with games. Everything from combat strategy to resource management has rules and outcomes. We often think

FIRST Robotics participants compete to build the best robots.

of games as fun, but things like military strategy can have important and life-changing results. For example, instead of putting people in cockpits to fly planes, pilots fly remote-controlled drones and watch the bombs drop in other countries without ever leaving the ground.

Meaningful Games: Games to Make People and the World Better

Some games are created to help solve important problems while still being fun and challenging. These games encourage meaningful play. Foldit is a virtual game where players manipulate or "fold" human proteins into patterns to try to create cures for diseases such as HIV/AIDS, Alzheimer's, and cancer. Scientists asked game players to help them because the players are so good at finding complex patterns. In just 10 days players solved one problem that had stumped scientists for 15 years!

FIRST Robotics is a worldwide robotics competition. Student teams build a robot to compete in a specific task, such as shooting a ball into a hoop. The game changes every year, and the teams have only two months to design, build, and test their robots.

The Come Out & Play Festival turns New York City into a big playground for adults to play games like kids play at camp. And just like at summer camp, the real point of the games is to make friends and connect with people.

Chapter 3

The Mind of a Designer

OK, so you want to be a great game designer? Game designers combine the skills of mind readers and scientists. Like mind readers, they have to read the emotions and responses of game players. Like scientists, they design systems that make people feel emotions and want to keep playing. Here are lessons that game designers all learn:

Failure Is Your Best Friend

Sometimes failure is a bad word in school. It means you didn't do what you were supposed to do. But game design is different, and so is life. In game design, failure is OK. Failure leads to learning. It also leads to progress. Failure eventually leads to success. Ask any successful person, and they will tell you the same thing. Treat failure as your new best friend.

Studying classic games such as chess can help you improve your own game designs.

Play Lots of Games and Think Critically About Them

Just sitting in front of a screen and playing obsessively won't help you grow as a game designer. But thoughtful play, where you think about why you are engrossed in or bored by a game, teaches you valuable lessons about good game design. Learn

Ask your family and friends what they like and don't like about different games.

from your gaming experiences. You can tell your parents you read it in a book.

Talk to People About Your Game—All the Time

Very few ideas come from only one brain. You have a team of thinkers around you: friends, family, a social network, and teachers. Everyone is rooting for you to become great. The world will help you succeed if you let it know what you're trying to do. If your world doesn't feel this way, then go somewhere where it does.

Learn to Love Criticism, Even If You Hate It

Designers begin with a powerful personal vision for their games, but they balance this vision with the **feedback** they get from others. After all, a game is no fun if you are the only person who wants to play it! It is hard to learn to take feedback, but without it you will never become a great designer. Some feedback is positive: "Wow! I stayed up all night playing that!" Other feedback is critical: "The game was so boring that I couldn't even finish it." No game will be perfect to every person, but listen carefully for patterns in the criticisms you get. Consider those patterns carefully, and your good game could become great!

Write It Down

When we're in imagination mode, we think that we'll remember our ideas forever. But later, when we have time to work on our game, we find that our ideas have slipped away. Many creative people carry a pocket-sized notebook or index cards and a pencil so they can capture their ideas when they come.

Write down your ideas as soon as you think of them.

Ask a Game Designer

When I show other people my game, they either don't get it or tell me to change it. I like my game as is. What should I do?

It may be hard to believe, but you actually want people to criticize your game. Getting feedback so that you can improve is the main thing game designers do. Coming up with an idea for a game is quick and easy in comparison. You don't want feedback from friends, family, or even anyone who already knows you. Why? Because it's hard to tell a friend his game stinks. If you have only friends play your game, you'll never get the truth. When I have people test my games, the first question I like to ask them is, "What don't you like about the game?" This is followed up with, "Why?" At first, it was difficult for me to hear criticism of my games, and I didn't always listen as well as I should have. Now that I do, my games are better than ever.

David Whitcher runs Protospiel, an annual event where board game designers meet and test their new games. He has published many board and card games through his company, PyroMyth Games.

Chapter 4

Make a Game, Level 1

You might be able to use pieces from other games to design your project.

Now you know the designer's mind-set. Let's get some glue, craft sticks, glitter, and . . . Ha! Just kidding! You don't need any of that stuff to make a game. There is no one guaranteed way to come up with a great game idea. **Inspiration** for games comes from many places, but let's try this to see if we can come up with a cool idea.

Finding Inspiration

First, clear a table, or make a blank space on a wall. Ask a few friends to come and join you. Browse a bunch of magazines or search the Internet. Take 15 minutes to collect at least 10 examples of things that make you think, "That looks really cool or beautiful or interesting." Gather as many examples as you can: photographs, statues, drawings, styles, or anything else. You can pull these items from any source, including comics, games, or the outdoors. If possible, print or draw each example, and stick it up on a wall or lay it out on a table. If you are stuck and need help, go online to *www.cherrylakepublishing.com/links* for some inspiring links.

All done? Next, set a timer for 15 minutes. Make a list of at least 10 stories that made you feel strong emotions. You could have been happy, sad, amazed, excited, or frightened. It's up to you. The stories can come from books, movies, games, or your life.

You don't need to write the whole story, just the name or a few words so you remember what it is. Add the stories to your wall or table.

Got that? Great! Now you have 15 minutes to write down at least 10 of your favorite games. They could be board games, video games, sports, or anything else you can think of. Add the games to your wall or table.

Now we have examples of your favorite designs, stories, and games. Choose one item from each group and ask the following question, "What if I made a game that played like (game), had a storyline like (story), and used a theme similar to (design)?"

What if you made a game that you played like Monopoly with a storyline like *The 39 Clues* using a theme similar to Harry Potter? What would it look like? How would it be different than the original game? Would it be fun? What would make it fun? Do those three elements work well together?

If you don't like a combination, try another one. Keep mixing and matching until you have one or two combinations that you really like.

Keep in mind that very few games are completely original. Most new games build on older games. That's why playing games is so important. You're creating a library of games, stories, and designs in your brain for your next project. If you can't come up with a game idea right now, that's OK. Just keep thinking, playing, and saving ideas in your notebook!

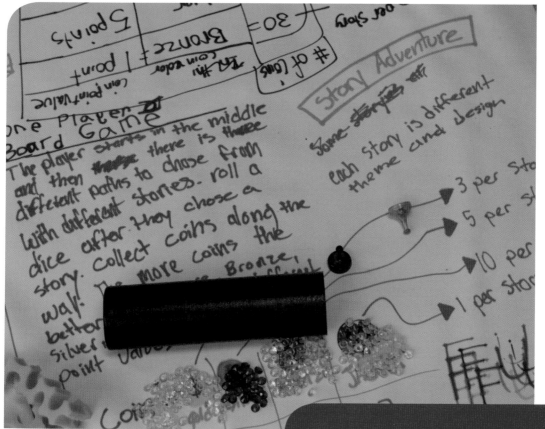

Write down the rules of your game as you plan out your ideas.

Chapter 5

Make a Game, Level 2

O K, you have a game idea. Maybe it came from the previous chapter, or maybe you had it before you even opened this book. Now what?

Refine = Think + Prototype + Test

Refine. To **refine** something means to make it better. Your goal now is to turn your rough game idea into a real game that people can play and enjoy. There's more than one way to do it and no specific order to do it in, but it always involves lots of thinking and testing.

Think. As you refine and test you'll find new problems to think through and solve. Your game may be too easy (boring) or too hard (frustrating). The game mechanics may be broken. The spin wheel may get stuck. If you can't find the right solution even after hours of thought, don't worry. It happens to all game designers! Ask someone for advice.

A prototype doesn't look like a finished game, but it can be played and tested.

Go for a walk or do something else, and then come back to your game later. Your brain will figure out a solution if you keep trying and don't give up.

Prototype. A **prototype** is like a first draft. It is a rough version of your game made quickly. Prototypes don't necessarily look pretty. Their only purpose is to let you test the basic idea of a game so you can discover

Ask a Game Designer

My game plays pretty well, but there's one part that everyone complains about. I really like that part, though! I think I know how to fix it, but I don't really want to. Any thoughts?

The hardest thing about designing games is letting go. When you first start to design a game, you want to add as many things as you can, trying to make it the most awesome thing ever. But when you take it out for a spin, some things just don't work. And others, well, they kind of work, but they could be better. So you start tinkering, making little changes, and trying again. There are even times when you have to completely redo major parts of your game again and again until you get it right. While it is hard to let go of all those pieces that didn't work, in the end you are left with this pure and beautiful thing that brings other people happiness.

Brian Mayer brings game design to kids through libraries and schools. His cooperative game is about the abolitionist movement and the Underground Railroad.

Play your game over and over to see what works and what needs to be changed.

what works and what doesn't. Prototypes might be made out of paper and tape, even though you imagine the finished product as laminated cards or even a video game. Most game designers create many prototypes.

Test. To test your game means to play it with others and get feedback. Playing by yourself is useful, but playing your game with others is the real test. When you're testing, you're like a detective. Look for clues that tell you if people are having fun. If they are not having fun, try to figure out what isn't working. Once you have those clues, you can rethink, make a new prototype, and test again. Remember to keep an open mind while testing and always thank people who help test your game.

Start!

Congratulations! You've made it to the end of this book, but this is just the beginning of the road to becoming a game designer. There's so much more to know. Go to *www.cherrylakepublishing.com/links* to get more resources to help you on your journey.

You could make the next Minecraft. You could design the next Settlers of Catan. You could come up with the next game that every kid likes to play. Along the way, you'll learn what makes great games great, have fun with your friends, and enjoy giving your imagination a workout.

So be excited. Stay excited. Go think, try, fail, test, design, prototype, share, document, discuss, refine, watch, model, build, change, listen, and most of all . . . *play!*

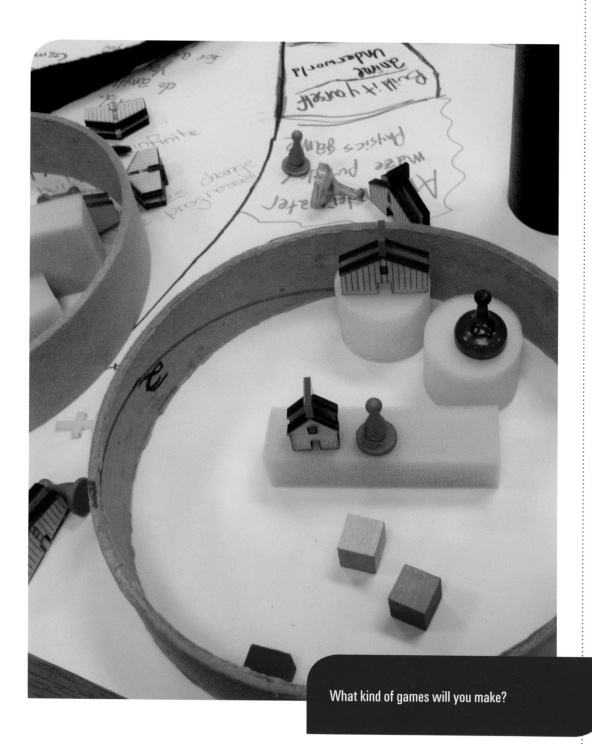

What kind of games will you make?

Glossary

feedback (FEED-bak) information and reactions about an item, action, or process

incentives (in-SEN-tivz) things that make a person try or work harder

inspiration (in-spuh-RAY-shuhn) something that encourages a person or provides ideas

outcomes (OUT-kuhmz) the results of actions or events

prototype (PROH-tuh-tipe) an early version of an invention that is used to test ideas

refine (ri-FINE) to improve or perfect something

strategies (STRAT-uh-jeez) clever plans for achieving a goal

tactics (TAK-tiks) methods of achieving a goal

Find Out More

BOOKS

Harbour, Jonathan S. *Video Game Programming for Kids*. Boston: Cengage Learning, 2012.

Taggar, Sam, and Susan Williamson. *Great Games: Old and New, Indoor, Outdoor, Ball, Board, Card & Word*. Nashville, TN: Williamson Publishing Company, 2004.

WEB SITE

First Steps in Board Game Design
http://edweb.sdsu.edu/courses/edtec670/boardgame /BoardGameDesign1.html
Check out some helpful hints for making board games.

Index

About the Author

Greg Austic is an open technology advocate, game designer, and researcher at Michigan State University.